"Power is available for your use, and the connection also is ready, but it is up to you to turn on the switch."

You can become your own best self only by remaining true to yourself. There is a clear and simple path to self-discovery, as beautiful and direct as a straight line.

Jessie K. Crum speaks of inspirational listening through which she discovered and freed the soul of a poet—her own. In this fascinating book she explores her personal experiences, showing how, when and why she was able to tap heretofore unimagined wisdom, grace, even genius, which in her case found its expression in writing.

Here is a touchstone to perception beyond the conscious mind; toward an integrated and harmonious wholeness of mind and spirit. . . .

"Every man is potentially creative, and the seeds of genius are asleep within him."

THE ART OF
INNER LISTENING

Pathway to Creativity

JESSIE K. CRUM

QUEST BOOKS   WHEATON, ILLINOIS

THE ART OF INNER LISTENING

A Quest Book

Fourth printing, 1989

ISBN: 0-8356-0303-2

Library of Congress Catalog Card Number: 74-21643

Printed in the United States of America

QUEST BOOKS are published by
The Theosophical Publishing House
Wheaton, Illinois 60187 U.S.A.

AN APPRECIATION

To friends, teachers, and members of my family, whose understanding and encouragement have been a source of inspiration and help in writing this book, as well as in my personal search for self-understanding, I am deeply grateful.

Among those to whom I owe an especial debt of gratitude is my beloved daughter-in-law, Faye E. Crum, who spent many hours helping me select and arrange the material from my many notebooks.

Others to whom I owe appreciation and thanks are my friends, Dr. and Mrs. H. Douglas Wild, Mrs. Helen Stinar, and Mrs. Terri Pinckard, for reading the manuscript and for helpful suggestions.

CONTENTS

PART ONE: DISCOVERY

PART TWO: CREATIVITY IS YOUR BIRTHRIGHT

PART THREE: STEPS ON THE PATHWAY

PART ONE: DISCOVERY

As you refine the channels through which thought flows it becomes more like its original essence. When you make the effort to purify and refine thought the wave of love from the Creator reaches you in comparative purity and the lower self can recognize its true relationship to the Higher Self, the *inner you*. Undesirable thoughts and habits will *cure* themselves as veils of illusion drop away. The *inner you* is not some strange spiritual being, far removed and unapproachable. Recognize this truth and let the *inner you* become the center of your complete and fully functioning self.

CHAPTER 1

Introduction

So you would like to be a genius!

As with all forms of greatness, a price must be paid for such an achievement. It cannot be accomplished overnight. But it *is* possible to awaken and develop your creative powers to a far greater extent than may seem possible as you read these opening words. This book sets forth a method—essentially simple but requiring confidence and persistence—for opening a vital channel between the everyday you and an area of being of which most of us are not ordinarily aware and from which we needlessly cut ourselves off through our preoccupation with the mundane affairs of life. It is an aspect of ourselves which contains undreamed-of potential, not only for our own more effective living but also for the wisdom to help our fellow pilgrims through times of stress.

Every one of us is at some time confronted with the necessity for making important decisions, decisions which may irrevocably turn our life in one direction or

another. At such times we desperately need answers—
not the facile answers of expediency but those which
spring from a wisdom in harmony with spiritual law.*
Such answers seem to come more readily to some individuals than to others, for they have been able—often
perhaps without knowing it—to tap a level of awareness which exists in every one of us and which, if we
can establish contact with it, leads to the development
of our creative potential and the deepening and
strengthening of our spiritual life.

This level of awareness corresponds with what some
call intuition, that faculty of understanding, perception,
and discernment, or direct knowing, which exists at a
level beyond the conscious, reasoning mind. Rooted in
wholeness, intuition acts as a mirror to reflect itself into
consciousness through thought. Although unfragmented
and perfect at its source, this inner knowing may be
distorted by the personality-centered individual. It is
well therefore to free ourselves so far as possible from
rigidities of temperament and from the conditioning of
our environment.

Many years ago, in a time of personal trauma, I discovered the possibility of getting help from this inner
level of the self. Overwhelmed by indecision and despair, I turned inward and asked, "What shall I do
now?" Thinking stopped momentarily, and I listened.
Suddenly, a clear, compelling thought flooded my
mind, answering my question and bringing insight into
my personal responsibility for the exigency which was
causing emotional and mental anguish.

Thereafter, whenever threatened by especially stress-
ful situations, or when faced by indecision and doubt,
I turned within for help. If I listened intently, my
mind stilled, there arose from this tranquil silence in response to my questions, a degree of self-understanding

---

* In this book "spiritual" indicates inner harmony and balance.

through lucid, concise thought. This practice was used at first only for emergencies and was not connected with my daily meditations.

Later, in 1966, participating in a meditation group interested in experimenting along these lines, I began to practice inner listening regularly.

In the group situation, after each meditation, a question was asked by one or more members. Anyone wishing to take part in the exercise wrote the question, inwardly repeated it, and then listened with eyes closed to prevent sight-triggered thought-images. Any thoughts that came into consciousness were recorded. Surprisingly, answers received in this way on a particular question, although varied in style and content, were not contradictory. We seemed to be drawing on the same source of information, with each one reacting to it in a personal and individual way.

This was not automatic writing—no one heard voices: nothing mediumistic occurred. Each one was fully cognizant of his own thoughts. One began to wonder if it were really possible, through this method, to tap a depth of understanding unknown and unused by most of us.

I had meditated for many years, hoping to learn eventually to still my mind. According to both religious and yogic disciplines, mental quietude is important for attainment of understanding that reaches beyond the realm of reason. But for me the concept of stilling the mind through meditation remained unclear, and I was far from sure what it would or would not do for me once I achieved it. I assumed it would enable me to live as a supportive, contributing member of society.

However, meditation had given me a recognizable degree of emotional serenity and control, and I reminded myself that this should be compensation enough. But, stillness? . . . peace? The harder I tried, the more remote success appeared. Mind, instead of becoming still, raced teasingly from thought to thought, defying my efforts to control it. With such a background of frustration and failure in reaching inner stillness, I now asked myself if the listening technique with which we were experimenting would enable anyone using it to still the mind. More importantly, would it result in reaching an archetypal level of intuition and creativity?

The method was simple, A child could use it. Inwardly ask a question: then listen intently, *really listen.* I realized that this was the same procedure that previously had proved effective in times of singular need. The only difference was the use of a notebook for recording questions and answers.

I began to practice inner listening at home each morning after meditation. This proved to be rewarding in many ways. The link between inner and outer mind seemed stronger. Information which I could not recall having heard or read before flowed into my mind. In response to questions, the meanings of symbolic dreams, of ancient legends, and of sacred scriptures became clear. Personal, unresolved inner conflicts and hidden motives were revealed. I could observe them rationally without feelings of guilt, and I felt that I was gaining more self-understanding. It was an exciting and stimulating experience. I was eager to continue this adventure into the "inner space" of self.

In taking the reader through the steps of the experiment, it will be necessary to use—and perhaps overuse—the pronoun "I." But it is understood that, while each of us is unique in manner of expression and even in ways of interpreting experience, all are rooted in a universal spiritual reality. And everyone who has ever given the matter conscious thought longs for a richer, fuller, and more meaningful life. It is to this end that my individual discoveries are shared.

CHAPTER 2

A Search For Understanding

I continued to perfect the technique of *inner listening*. As I *tuned in* more and more to this inner mind, I experienced deeper levels of understanding. Sometimes, in reading a book, I discovered new depths of meaning and significance.

A sense of inner joy has been one of the plus values I have found in my search for self-understanding and contact with inner levels of mind. In this quest, my questions have ranged from sublime to trivial, and even to the ridiculous. As an example, a more *weighty* type of questioning concerned the nature of *truth*.

"Is Truth," I asked, "changeless and eternal? We constantly speak of *Truth* and the need to find and know it. For what are we looking? Or is truth something that may be glimpsed, but never grasped? Does one become aware of what truth is little by little, or does it come like a flash of light or an inner awakening?"

Briefly I contemplated the questions I had written,

15

and then I stopped thinking and just listened—listened as intently as if my very life depended upon hearing some far distant sound. Suddenly, answers to my questions entered the threshold of consciousness, and I recorded them in my notebook:

"If you could take knowledge, and add to it wisdom and understanding, you would begin to know something of the meaning of truth. Do not look for truth with a capital T. Search for something less elusive and of more immediate value to you. Look rather for the truth about yourself. Just how well do you know yourself? How do you feel about yourself, and how do you relate to other individuals? They, like you, have problems, fears, anxieties, frustrations, hopes, joys, and longings for completeness

"You wish for understanding to discover truth? Then, be aware that self-knowledge is the beginning of understanding. Without understanding how can you expect to find truth? Many people in a vague way are looking for truth. They dream, also, of some day *doing good* in the world. Such ideas for most individuals are unformulated and tenuous, slumbering in hidden recesses of the mind. These dimly perceived longings may be expressed by *wishing* for money or time to use in *helping people*. Such wishful thoughts are of no more use than evanescent dreams. To help others you must first have sufficient understanding to help yourself. If you can help yourself, if you can understand yourself, then you will be ready to help those who may need your help, and who perchance may accept the help offered."

The flow of thought stopped. It was as if some inner part of myself had spoken, not with audible words, but with clear and concise thoughts. It was as if this *inner mind* spoke with authority and sure knowledge. I had written the thoughts as they flowed into my *outer mind*. Now, I read and re-read what I had written in my notebook. Time seemed to stand still as I entered a state almost of reverie. The mask of maturity, for the moment, was pushed aside and I looked at myself in retrospect from childhood to youth, and on into maturity and age.

Again I turned my attention inward. "Is it possible for me truly to know and understand myself?" I asked. I listened, and the answer came:

"The personal self is a strong barrier to hold back and block the pathway to true knowledge and self-understanding. But it is possible. Personal discipline and much effort are required. Do not expect this to be an easy task."

✳ "How do I begin this search for self-understanding?" I inquired.

"You begin with self-examination of thought, emotion, and action. This brings understanding as to why you think, feel, and act as you do.

"If you find yourself becoming emotional about something (often trivial or inconsequential in nature), stop and inwardly ask yourself, 'What is the reason for this? Why am I feeling as I do?' Then listen to what the *inner you* can tell you. This can help prevent emotional build-up with its resulting loss of vital force and energy, and may allow the *inner you* to reveal some hidden motive or causative factors that will help you regain emotional balance."

Then I asked, "Are there books I could read which would be helpful?" Again came an answering thought:

"Books have been written that can point the way and give useful hints. Systems and methodologies have been offered by many religions, philosophies, and teachers. Much is available and some will prove helpful, but all these are but steps leading to the ocean of truth and understanding. Each one, in the end, must find his own inner awareness of truth. Into the ocean one must plunge and leave behind the stepping stones."

While continuing the effort to establish deeper and more meaningful contact with Higher Mind, I asked if I were making progress, and if the thoughts coming to me really were from Higher Mind and not from lower mind. I received this answer:

"You have made some progress. Your aspirations are helpful; but aspiration is not enough. You need to make an effort for contact each day through meditation, listening, and writing. Consciousness at the personality level is not a perfect receiver. The magnetic thread which connects higher with lower mind is still weak and wavering. As you train and perfect the instrument of lower mind it will become a better reflector of Higher Mind. Write each day. This will help to strengthen the link.

"You are fearful that the messages you receive come from lower mind. Even though words are supplied by lower mind, the inspiration for them comes from Higher Mind. Be aware however, that lower mind can color, shade, or even distort messages, according to preconceived ideas and beliefs. This may be very slight if you strive to be impersonal and if you do not hold tenaciously to beliefs and dogmas that have influenced or colored your thinking.

"The lack of sureness as to authenticity of the source will pass when the connecting band is stronger. At present, it is like a fine thread strung from higher to lower mind, but it can, through use and effort, become a strong cord. Remember that electricity can flow over a small wire when the needed conditions are established, but the largest cable cannot supply electrical power unless it is connected with the source of power.

"Power is available for your use, and the connection also is ready, but it is up to you to turn on the switch. You can be sure that the magnetic link is even now strong enough to bring through into consciousness, understanding and knowledge from Higher Mind. You must believe that this is so, if you would go forward to greater understanding and usefulness. Disbelief, in itself, can turn off the power."

The message seemed clear enough, but I still felt there must be some magical or near-magical key that would make possible the transition from concrete, outer mind to the inspirational and creative level of Higher Mind. I considered this possibility and then asked: "Should I spend more time in meditation in order to make greater progress and to more easily contact Higher Mind?" Then came these answering thoughts:

"To make progress of any significance, you need to learn to meditate effectively. This, too, requires effort and perseverance. The time spent on this is not the important thing. You have other obligations to fulfill, and this, too, takes time each day. You need to have proper balance in your daily life. This includes time spent in meditation, in study, and in doing the daily tasks necessary because of your particular life situation.

"As you progress there is the possibility of instantaneous communication with Higher Self. The channel will widen and deepen as it is used, allowing for greater ease of communication. Also, the information received will be clearer and more truly perceived.

"When a would-be athlete, with little muscular coordination, starts to train, his beginning efforts show little result, but through daily practice, little by little, he brings about a transformation in himself. This is not unlike what happens in the attainment of self-understanding and contact with Higher Mind. It is the daily practice that works the transformation. Wishful thinking and occasional effort will bring little understanding or growth."

CHAPTER 3

Thought and Emotion Have Far-Reaching Effects

"Thought can be as beneficent as a gentle rain upon a parched and thirsty earth, or it can be like a tornado which destroys cities and forests and wrecks boats and ships in the usually safe harbors of the ocean." This came to me as I contemplated the complex field of thought and its effect upon the personal self and upon our world.

Members of the meditation group to which I belonged had been meditating upon thought and its far-reaching effects. We met each week for meditation and to share what we received through *inspirational listening*. The above quotation was one of my briefer contributions. However, one of our members came up with something entirely new to our thinking, but which impressed me more and more as I contemplated the message she gave our group. From her notebook she read:

"You ask what is thought?

"Thought is action on a higher plane of awareness. It is the soul's equivalent of an arm or hand. In a sense, it is mind's body. The resulting action on the physical plane is the manifestation of action on this higher plane. The soul, itself, is force. Thought, then, has to be the effect of force. Since man's consciousness is centered chiefly in the physical, he has great difficulty transplanting thought from dense matter to fields of force. But that is what true man really is, a field of force.[1]

"To better understand the nature and power of thought, we might compare it to electricity. The electricity used in your home is the effect of force. Man has learned to channel electricity for his use through switches and generators. Now, the brain of man can be likened to an electrical generator, and the mind to switches and relays; the resulting effect is current. This current of thought, like the current of electricity, can be constructive or destructive, depending upon how it is channeled through the personality. If too much current of incorrect voltage is used distortion or damage may result.

"If you can learn to channel exactly the right amount of mental current through your physical body at all times, perfect health will be the result. If you could channel the correct amount from you, a field of force would be built up about you, vivifying and refining the finer matter and charging it with the correct vibratory rate. This in turn would charge all the matter which it contacts to the proper rate. Now, thought is a specialized charge of this force and, properly directed, can restore and renew in perfection all matter which it penetrates.

"Thought power is dissipated through such emotions as worry, fear, envy, and despair. When you indulge in these emotions you drain away your supply of energy

---

[1] This was early in 1967, before release of information about Kirlian photography, which shows what appears to be force fields (coronas) around plant and animal forms.

and power. The result is not merely the loss of energy and health, but the pollution of the ocean of thought in which we all live.

"Continued misuse of thought power, reinforced by destructive emotions, in time builds up a field of static, which almost completely cuts off the Creator's force and contact with Higher Mind. To disperse this cloud of static, one needs to maintain inner balance. This is achieved through emotional control. If, constantly, you swing from high to low, you are wasting power. Each time you find emotion ruling you, determine why this is so. Each time the *inner you* regains command, it becomes easier to achieve control. Through continued practice of this kind, unwanted static gradually disappears. This also widens and deepens the channel from higher to lower mind. The final result: many personal benefits as well as valuable effects for those you contact. Can you not see that if enough people would practice thought and emotional control, the entire world, at long last, would begin to live in peace and harmony?"

Our group continued its effort to understand more about the far-reaching effects of thought and emotion. Some were reluctant to contribute, but all were interested in hearing what others had to say.

The remainder of this chapter is not all from my personal notebooks; some of it was "received" by the member quoted above. However, I shall dispense with quotation marks for the present and get on with the story of thought and emotion and their far-reaching effects as this became apparent to us through inspirational listening.

How Thought Originates

Thought begins as an expression of the Creator's love. As it filters through layers or planes of consciousness, it takes on qualities of each level. What started out as the pure expression of the Creator becomes polluted by what man has become at his lowest level. Here are to be found coarser thoughts and trivial ideas of many kinds. The higher mental body is the source of abstract, philosophical, and creative concepts.

It becomes obvious that thought does not enter personality awareness in original purity. It may be distorted, somewhat like a picture out of focus. It is difficult to receive thoughts from Higher Mind if lower mind is cluttered with trivia. It is even more difficult if emotional turmoil distorts and blurs the true picture or message. However, as you refine the channel, results achieved are clearer and closer to original essence.

The lower mental body draws into itself thoughtforms from other *thinkers*. These may be vague and relatively harmless, or vicious and harmful. Countless thoughts of all kinds are sent out from the minds of men. Some of these are intensified by emotions of fear, guilt, prejudice, hate, and anger. These become powerful poisons in the great ocean of mental matter. The end result can be sickness, destruction, and violence for mankind.

Needed today are those who can and will use the power of proper thought to combat this evil, and who, like knights of old, will fight against dragons of fear, ignorance, superstition, and hate, which are created by wrong thought and emotion and sent forth upon their destructive course. This evil can be transmuted only through correct and proper thinking by many individuals. As each one succeeds in becoming a channel for pure thought, the World Consciousness will be purified and renewed.

No one can assume that he is blameless for the discord and violence prevalent today. Each one, according to the power and quality of his thinking and feeling, is responsible for the present situation. The misuse of thought and its resulting emotion has built a world which threatens to topple us all into an abyss of darkness and despair.

You ask, "How can we change and rebuild the world into a place of harmony and peace where a truly good life can become a reality?"

There is a way. Each one must accept personal responsibility for his own misuse of thought and begin to make proper application of it. What improper thought has destroyed, proper thought can rebuild. Every individual can help to create a world of harmony and peace if he will begin to retrain his thought process; and with proper thought will come right action. Harmony within will manifest as harmony without. It is of paramount importance to be aware of thought and its far-reaching effect.

This matter of thought and emotional control is not a process of giving up or killing out undesirable thoughts and emotions. You are training yourself to give control to the *real you*. Achievement does not result from the separation of lower from higher. When you separate the two parts of the true unity of being, you weaken the effectiveness of the whole. Just as fingers of the hand cannot function as well separately as when joined with the thumb, so Higher Self cannot function as effectively unless joined with lower self, symbolically the thumb. By giving control to the higher portion of yourself, you, through active cooperation, are refining and changing the thought patterns of lower self.

Thought, which started out as an expression of the Creator's love, can become polluted and distorted. As you refine the channels through which thought flows, it becomes more like its original essence. When you make the effort to purify and refine thought, the wave of love from the Creator reaches you in comparative purity, and the lower self can recognize its true relationship to

Higher Self, the *inner you*. Undesirable thoughts and habits will *cure* themselves as veils of illusion drop away. This *inner you* is not some strange spiritual being, far removed and unapproachable. Recognize this truth and let the *inner you* become the center of your complete and fully functioning self.

When you think about a thing of goodness or beauty or a thing of evil and destruction, you give it added force and power in direct proportion to the strength and power of your thought and feeling. Can you not see that this gives renewed life and influence to all such forces?

If you would reduce violence and destruction, think upon their opposites. Instead of visualizing the misdeeds of violent people and decrying their evil ways, center your thought upon the opposite forces which work for the upliftment of humanity. Send out thoughts of peace, of harmony, and of right action. Direct this powerful force for good into the World Consciousness, that to some extent it may be given this positive influence.

Even though no immediate result can be seen, you may be sure there are constructive effects. Such positive thoughts are like a clear stream of pure water flowing into a great, turbid river. At the point of entry there is a pool of relatively pure water, and when many such streams are entering the river it is renewed and purified.

When you think on things positive for good you are creating a pool of pure thought that has power to influence others in your mental atmosphere. When many individuals are likewise engaged in such constructive thinking, the inner worlds of thought and emotion will be rebuilt into a new and harmonious wholeness that will have a beneficial and dynamic effect in the outer world in which men and women live, and work, and hope. We then will begin to see a world of peace, harmony, and beauty. The mainstream of thought gradually will be purified and revitalized with the living waters of spiritual blessing and true understanding. Let your thought and emotion be for the uplifting of mankind and for the perfecting of the world about you.

In the words of Saint Paul, ". . . whatsoever things are honest, whatsoever things are just, whatsoever things are pure, whatsoever things are lovely, whatsoever things are of good report; if there be any virtue, and if there be any praise, think on those things."[2]

---

[2] Phil. 2:8

PART TWO:
CREATIVITY IS YOUR BIRTHRIGHT

. . . All so-called creative individuals make use of the faculty of Higher Mind, either consciously or unconsciously. It is not just the genius who has a creative mind. All have creativity in latency and, through effort, latent creative genius can be nurtured and brought into actuality. All have the ability to be creative when the inner wisdom of Higher Mind is brought through into consciousness. (p. 34)

CHAPTER 4

You Are Potentially Creative

Every man is potentially creative, and the seeds of genius are asleep within him. If this is true it must be because of the operation of fundamental, natural law, otherwise it is only wishful thinking to say that man has the gift of creativity as his birthright.

Let us go for a moment to the Christian Bible to make a point: "And the Lord God formed man of the dust of the ground, and breathed into his nostrils the breath of life; and man became a living soul."[1] Here is a brief, allegorical story of the creation of man.

It is true that the body of man is composed of the same substances as those found in water, stone, and soil, designed by the Creator in an intricate and perfect pattern. But man was not truly *man* until the Creator breathed into him "the breath of life." This "breath of life" from the Creator is the true source of man's birth

---
[1] Gen. 2:7

as *man,* for the essence of his being is this breath or spark of the very self of the Creator.

The essence and life of God, the Creator, is therefore within every man. It is for this reason that man can speak to God and know that his very thoughts are heard. The truth is that man is magnetically linked with the Creator by this breath or spark. Also, this oneness with God is the reason why every man is potentially a creative being. This is his birthright, but only by virtue of being the son or daughter of the Most High God, one with him in creative, spiritual essence. This essence is *true* man in his innermost being. Spiritual vibration, or "the breath of life," has made him man, but he must act through the personality complex of physical body, emotions, and concrete mind. Despite this inner link with the Creator, the mind of man is so occupied with its own relatively trivial thoughts that it is unable to keep still long enough to *listen in* to the wisdom and understanding which is available.

This inner, essential part of man is an ever-expanding, ever-deepening force field of power and perfection. It also pervades in essence the whole of creation, from the grain of sand to planetary systems, from the smallest creeping creature to the highest spiritual being. In man it can become creativity through thought and action.

Here, then, is the true basis for the brotherhood of man and the kinship of all life. It is the reason, also, for the quite generally accepted belief that God can hear and answer prayer.

All are children of destiny born for greatness, and can in this life begin to achieve the greatness which is the birthright of all. The greatness here referred to is an inner greatness of spirit. Each one is truly of the life and essence of the Creator and as such is the lineal heir to His greatness.

Why then does man walk in delusion and smallness

of spirit when he could walk upon the highroad of spiritual greatness? It is for each one to choose. Do we choose to serve the innermost God Self and work to make this earth a heavenly abode for all men? Or do we choose to walk upon the outermost fringe of the magnetic field of the Most High, so far removed from His peace and love that we forget there is anything except the outer garments of body, mind, and emotion?

This outermost self might be likened to a desert land. But within the gates of the City of Life is a pleasant land where the weary traveler will find beauty, peace, joy, and fulfillment. One can enter the portals of the city through the gateway of Higher Mind and know that one is truly a son or daughter of the Most High.

Once this vision is glimpsed and the reality of the true self is experienced, selfish striving falls away as autumn leaves drop from the trees. As a tree is more than leaves and branches but has trunk and roots, so also is man more than the visible outer self. The reality of each individual ever remains. Each one is a leaf upon the tree of life, and all have inner unity and kinship.

Since the center and core of man is this atom or force of the Creator, inner levels of mind are closely attuned to the creative essence. But only as one learns to reach this level of awareness (Higher Mind) does one become capable of creative thought and work. To understand why this is so, one must be aware that this inner level of man is a highly complex field of force and for its expression requires finer matter than is generally contained in the personality structure of the average person.

This outer individuality consists of three components. First, and most obvious, is the active and demanding physical body which clamors for action, for food, for sensation, for rest and sleep. There is also the emotional factor which generates a force field of its own. This emotional force field in the average individual is made up of relatively coarse vibratory matter. The love of the Creator at this level is difficlut to recognize as having started out from a *heavenly* source. Emotions of anger, hatred, jealousy, irritation, worry, impatience, etc., can and do generate vast amounts of static, which in turn become an all but impenetrable barrier. It is difficult, if not impossible, for the creative potential to manifest until there is refining and clearing of this force field.

There is another barrier that can prevent vibrations of Higher Mind from entering personal awareness. This is lower mind itself, which is ceaselessly occupied with thoughts of its body, its desires, and its prejudices. Man has accepted many ready-made ideas and beliefs about almost everything that has to do with his world. He has been conditioned by his total environment to such a degree that, indeed, there is a veritable mountain to be climbed before he can become aware of his problems. Should he manage to do this, then must come an important decision: does he really want to make the effort to become that which he has the inner potential to be? Should he decide that this is for him the only right and true way of life, then let him be aware that the way is long and difficult. Indeed, this is the age-old story of man's search for himself. It is the quest for the Holy Grail.

This is a search that may take many lives. To some the goal may seem to be reached quickly, but who can say how long the search may have lasted, or how great the effort in previous earthly lives? Do not be disturbed by the element of time. More important by far is complete dedication to the task. When the moment of utter dedication comes, the time of fulfillment will be close at hand.

CHAPTER 5

How To Contact Higher Mind

Do you wish to gain access to higher levels of awareness through contact with Higher Mind? The way is open to you. The degree of accomplishment will be in direct proportion to the effort made. A little effort, a little progress; much effort, greater progress. It is the same today as it has been in the past. The tried and true methods of approach are as effective now as when the prophets of old were "spoken to" by God. For the truth is, inner levels of consciousness speak to man with divine authority.

To some have come flashes of inspiration, of understanding, or wisdom, which may or may not have been repeated. But this is not the kind of communication that can be depended upon for daily and hourly help, inspiration, and guidance.

If you would contact Higher Mind remember that daily, regular effort is important. Lower mind is magnetically linked with Higher Mind, but this link can only be made stronger through use. If any results are forthcoming there must be more than brief, spasmodic effort. A few minutes or hours today, followed by days or weeks of doing nothing, will bring little if any results. Consistent, daily effort is required. If this is done, never doubt your ultimate success. He who would reach the temple of Higher Mind must work faithfully and steadily toward that end with daily regularity.

The seeker will find that there is already available much helpful information. Books have been written which can give some assistance, and there are men and women in the world today who have made progress along the path of inner development, who will give aid to the sincere seeker ready for such guidance.

There is also available to each individual his own greater Self, his own Higher Mind. Remember this is not from some faraway, outside source that you are seeking aid, but from your very own Innermost Self, who is ever ready and willing to help if the outer you will make this possible.

In times of need many have discovered this source of power, strength, and wisdom. It is unfortunate that few seek it except in moments of supreme need, for it is ever available, ever near. If one believes there is such an inner center of help and strength which can be contacted, or if perchance one discovers it in a time of need, then it is possible to set out upon the adventure of making this a known experience, an intimate part of daily living.

When you have an important decision to make, does your mind go round and round in ceaseless activity without reaching a conclusion? Do you, all too often, find yourself sitting on the fence of indecision wondering what course of action to take? Such mental merry-go-rounds can become a treadmill of repetitious thought which results in confusion and even greater indecision.

There is a way to avoid such time-consuming and

futile dilemmas. When you find yourself in a quandary of indecision, think the problem through from every angle which presents itself. Then write down all the ideas which come to you. Write, also, any questions you may have regarding the matter. After this, inwardly ask this deeper level of mind to help you make a wise decision. Then stop all thinking and remain as mentally still as possible for a brief time. Then write any thoughts which may come in answer to your questions. If no thoughts are forthcoming at the time, do not be disturbed, and above all do not begin to worry the mind with the problem like a dog with a bone. Stop thinking about the matter by mentally turning to other things. Wait until you are ready for bed. Then again write any questions you may have regarding the decision you need to make. Ask that understanding be given you while asleep so that when you awake you will know what action to take. Be sure to have beside your bed, easily within reach, a writing pad and pencil. Sometimes the answer may come during the night, waking you from sleep; or it may come in a dream. If this happens, do not return to sleep assuming you will be able to remember in the morning, but at once make the effort to write it in your notebook. If you wait until morning you may be unable to recall what seemed very clear during the night.

Possibly, you will sleep through the night and when you awake you may be unaware that an answer has been given to you while asleep and dreaming. But do not bound out of bed and start your usual day of activity. Take a few deep breaths. Then ask Higher Mind to give you the understanding you need, while maintaining a relaxed, expectant attitude. Now you are ready to receive your answer. Take up your paper and pencil and read your question or questions, directing them to this inner level of mind. Close your eyes and listen for the answer which will come as thought, not as a voice in your head; that is definitely to be avoided. Maintain a positive listening attitude, not a negative and passive one. Listen intently. This is important. If you focus your entire attention upon listening, the outer mind will not be engaged in *thinking*. It will be still. Even the closing of the eyes is for the purpose of preventing thoughts being triggered by the sense of sight.

When the first thought comes begin to write, even if it is but one word. There will probably be a flow of words. If so, continue to write as long as thought flows. Do not change the thought in any way. Your outer mind must now act as a receiving station for thoughts which come from Higher Mind. This outer mind with which you are so familiar is a useful servant, but its capacities are limited. But fortunately for us all, there is this deeper level of awareness which can be tapped and used. It is through Higher Mind that we can reach intuitive levels of understanding.

When you ask the Innermost Self for an answer to a question, listen with full expectation of receiving, and when an answering thought comes into consciousness believe that you have been answered and accept your answer. Many "hear" but do not believe that the "voice" (thought) comes from Higher Mind, and so neither write down the message nor attempt to carry out the instruction received.

Do not expect to hear an audible voice.

The "still, small voice" of the Innermost Self comes as thought, but this *thought* is not generated in the restless, outer garment of the mind. It arises out of a source of wisdom of which the concrete mind is unaware. It comes from the interior depth of being, and communicates its wisdom to the personality when the personal mind becomes still enough to listen.

Many individuals assume that nothing can be done about controlling the mind, but this is not true. Lower mind can be trained to be a good, if not a perfect instrument for receiving wise counsel and intuitive understanding from this inner or higher level of mind. The outer mind can become like a pool of still water, mirroring and reflecting the inner radiance of Higher Mind.

There is nothing strange or mysterious about this. All so-called creative individuals make use of this faculty of Higher Mind, either consciously or unconsciously. It is not just the genius who has a creative mind. All have this creative mind in latency and, through effort, latent creative genius can be nurtured and brought into actuality. All have the ability to be creative when the inner wisdom of Higher Mind is brought through into consciousness.

You may ask why more people do not discover and use this creative faculty? The reason is obvious: we are so busily engaged in the treadmill of our so-called *thinking* that we fail to reach inward to the real *thinker*, the creative mind that can give true understanding and enlightenment.

Some who aspire to contact Higher Mind fail to do so except on rare occasions, not because of any lack of ability, but only because they are unwilling to practice the needed self-discipline. Right motives and true effort cannot fail, but without real effort little progress can be made. Make no mistake about it, self-discipline and effort are required.

An infant is not concerned about its growth. Nature takes care of the child's growth patterns. But when a mature individual enters upon the path of personal unfoldment leading to self-knowledge and hastened progress, much effort is required. One cannot say, "This little thing will not count." Everything counts and is inwardly recorded and makes easier or more difficult the next step upon the pathway, according to the quality and nature of the effort made. Little by little and day

by day you can build into your life the qualities needed
for complete success.

Rearranging Lower Mind

It is important to set aside time each day for stilling
outer mind. This gives higher levels of mind an opportunity to reach personality consciousness. It also has
the beneficial effect of stopping the build-up of a mis-
cellaneous "junk pile" of useless mental furniture
which prevents any true or clear thinking. When the
outer mind is in a constant turmoil of activity it might
be likened to a room into which one continues to pile
all kinds of furniture, without thought as to its usefulness or appropriateness. It is as if a large and spacious
room were filled with an assortment of furniture of
every kind, with many small gadgets lying about in
every conceivable place. Such a room, containing a
disorderly conglomerate of things, is of little use for
any purpose.

Fortunately, there is something that can be done
about rearranging this room of lower mind. Higher
Mind can do this for you, provided the personality will
begin to use more control and stop cluttering the mind
with useless mental gadgets.

The clearing and rearranging of the mind is done
through emotional and mental control, for the two go
hand in hand. One helpful exercise is to set aside a
time each day for considering some needed quality such
as courage or perseverance. Relax as completely as
possible and keep the mind quietly upon the chosen
quality until a point is reached where nothing more of
interest can be added. Then stop all mental activity as
completely as possible and inwardly ask for help in ex-
emplifying the quality in daily life. Remain relaxed and
without strain throughout this exercise. It is important
not to be concerned over the success or failure of any

attempt *not to think*. At first inner stillness may be possible for only a few seconds. However, in this state of mind, time ceases to be of importance. If you wish to stop at a certain time, mentally affirm this at the beginning of the exercise. This will act as a mental alarm clock. In this exercise, also, a notebook should be kept to record anything which comes through into consciousness.

Remember that such communication must be channeled through lower mind and therefore can be twisted into something less than pure truth. Make no attempt to censor any thoughts that arise; neither should there be any effort to fit them into existing molds of opinion or belief. You must be willing to re-form your thinking.

Do not expect to be entirely successful, but be willing to try, and then to try again. Fear of failure, worry, and overeagerness to achieve are stumbling blocks that will delay progress, for they can build up *emotional static* to such an extent that higher levels of mind cannot penetrate into outer consciousness.

CHAPTER 6

I.Q. and Genius

It is said that only a fractional part of the mind is used by the average person. Some say that we use no more than one-tenth of our mental power. If an average man with an I. Q. (Intelligence Quotient) of 100 uses one-tenth of his mental power, possibly a man with a higher I. Q. would use a higher percentage of his mental capability. Such a person might be considered gifted or superior in intelligence. Still, a high percentage of his mind power is still floating about unused. Here is an undiscovered ocean whose vast depth has not been plumbed by the travelers of time and space called men and women.

This concept is thought-provoking. What are we doing with the unused eighty-five or ninety percent of our mental potential? Why do we not try to tap this additional source of wisdom and intelligence? If it is true that we have these unused mental resources, they must be available could we but find some way to reach them.

There have been in the past and are today creative individuals who in many fields of endeavor—music, the arts, mathematics, sciences, etc.—have outstripped the average man or woman. These creative persons may or may not be endowed with superior levels of intelligence which can be measured and certified by a psychologist. Creative individuals, in general, seem to be above average mentally. However, statistical studies offer no conclusive proof that this is true.

If a superior mentality is not the only true source of creative genius, what is the potent magic that brings it into manifestation? The scientifically oriented scholar might offer in explanation some fortuitous concourse of hereditary genes. The metaphysically oriented might contend that only reincarnation could adequately explain this anomaly of nature. He would point out that such a concourse of genes could only be activated for the soul who came to birth with a long background of lives dedicated to his particular creative discipline.

This last view appears reasonable, but few things have their roots in a single causative factor. Each of these projected reasons, in part, could be correct. Both views would effectively rule out the possibility of an average man or woman becoming a creative genius. Based on the premise of reincarnation alone, what a long, slow, uphill road looms before the man or woman of average, or even of above average, mentality who aspires to become a genius in any field of endeavor. Consider, also, the many lives and the tremendous effort needed to excel in more than one field. How many lives would be needed to excel in more than one field. Monumental labor would be required to reach the creative stature of a Leonardo da Vinci, who was not only a great artist, but also an engineer and scientist! What a long and weary road to emulate such a genius as Michelangelo, who considered himself first and foremost a sculptor, but who was equally great as painter and architect!

If a superior IQ is not the answer, and if reincarnation does not offer a definitive and complete solution, is there a key which will unlock the door to the enigma of creative genius?

I asked this question of the inner level of awareness that I call Higher Mind, and I received an answer. It was as if my known and familiar mind were a receiving station for a stream of fluent thought. It was meaningful and significant, and it flowed. There was no groping for words or apt phrases to express ideas, which is my usual pattern when writing. The answer to this and many other questions did not come at one session of writing, but over a period of time. What follows in this chapter, as well as in most of this book, is the result of such a flow of thought. There are, of course, transitional and explanatory passages, but much of it is transcribed from my notebook just as it came to me.

So you Want to be a Genius?

This book began with the question of whether you would like to be a genius and called attention to the fact that a price must be paid. If you are willing to pay that price, you can achieve the goal. For each individual has the superlative greatness of his own unique genius deeply hidden within his inmost being. To succeed in this search requires self-discipline and belief in oneself—and belief in the possibility of contacting levels of awareness that go a step beyond the logical, reasoning mind generally thought to be the only source of mental activity.

This is not to denigrate the importance of the concrete, outer mind. It has tremendous significance and needs to be developed and trained. Effective use of higher levels of mind requires a "receiving and transmitting station" which must be kept in good operating condition. It is therefore imperative that this outer mind, with which we are all so well acquainted, be subjected to the disciplines of study and research. Schools and colleges are designed for such training. But it must be recognized from the start that this outer mind is not the source of creativity and genius.

A musical genius such as Mozart does not suddenly begin to play and compose music without some previous training. Mozart played the harpsichord and composed music at the age of four and, when five, played three musical instruments. But his father, who was a skilled musician, noticed the child's great interest in music and began to teach him when the boy was three years old. This is the age when a child has what Madame Montessori terms an "absorbent mind" and easily learns and remembers one or more languages. Mozart died at thirty-six and might have failed to reach great musical genius had his training been postponed until much later.

The power to reach higher levels of creative mind is not something which is magically bestowed upon an occasional lucky individual; neither does it come through some happy coincidence or some whim of fate. There must be interest and desire in order to achieve. And then comes the need for training and daily practice. The first step is to *try*. To accomplish anything of importance requires effort. Results cannot be forthcoming unless there is first the effort to achieve the desired objective.

An infant does not learn to walk without making a great effort to do so. The success of the child is due to his constant and daily effort to stand upon his own small, unsteady feet. As the child tries, time and time again to pull himself upon his feet and stand alone, the muscles used become stronger and his balance is perfected. At last the day comes when he is able to stand alone. But still he has not learned to walk. There must be many faltering steps, many times when he will try and fail. He does not cease to try. He picks himself up and tries again and again.

Learning to use untried, innate mental powers requires much the same kind of effort that the child uses in learning to walk. Latent ability is activated through effort. Failure to achieve a desired objective today does not imply that success is impossible. To give up trying is the only failure. Know that even as the child learns to walk through effort and daily practice, so does an individual learn to contact and use the creative power of Higher mind.

Wishing is Not Enough

The man or woman who has creative genius has not received this as an unearned gift. Creative talent is developed through an effort to reach higher levels of awareness which are, indeed, part of every man's heritage. The higher faculties of mind are not available, however, merely by wishing for them. Wishing will not develop creativity.

The individual of sincere purpose will start as the child starts to walk. Each day he will use the "muscles" of the mind to develop the necessary strength for further effort. The first step, then, is simply stated in one word: TRY.

The line between success and failure is a narrow one. Constant awareness of this is needed. If the effort made today ends in failure, try again. Sometimes failure is not from trying too little, but is rather from trying too much. If, in the effort to succeed, one becomes emotional or is beset by worry and fear of failure, the result can be a kind of frenzied misuse of the whole energy field.

This is why it has been said that one must work with dispassion and without desire. It is this element of "desire" which can cause what has been termed "static" in the force field which surrounds every individual. Only when this force field is in a state of balance and harmony can you work with complete assurance of success. Overeagerness and desire to see results or receive rewards cause imbalance which builds up static to such a degree that it is all but impossible for deeper levels of awareness to penetrate the personality consciousness. This condition can be compared to trying to listen to a voice on the radio when the static is so great that the voice is distorted or completely blotted out.

CHAPTER 7

Finding The Kingdom Within

"And when he was demanded of the Pharisees, when the kingdom of God should come, he answered them and said, 'The kingdom of God cometh not with observation; Neither shall they say, Lo here! or, lo there! for behold, the kingdom of God is within you.' "[1]

What is the nature of this kingdom of God which is within you? It is the kingdom of Higher Mind and is close at hand. It can be reached by anyone who will make the effort to do so, but the effort must be made during your lifetime.

✗ It is not necessary to wait for some future incarnation when, hopefully, conditions will be more ideal, with fewer household or business obligations and commitments. The obstacles which now appear to be almost insurmountable may be essential for development of some needed quality necessary for reaching this inner kingdom. Intellectual brillance is not required;

[1] Luke 17:20-21

46

neither is it necessary to set immediate goals beyond present ability to attain. As skill is gained in small things, more difficult tasks can be undertaken with full expectation of ultimate success. This you can rely upon, for the infinite forces of the Creator's love, light, and wisdom flow through you and are available to all who seek.

What takes place may well be compared to music which can be heard when radio or television is turned on and tuned in. But first, there must be an instrument, and it must be turned on and the channel tuned in before the music can be heard. The personality of body, emotions, and mind is your instrument. When you reach up to Higher Mind you turn on the "switch" which connects you to the channel. And you might say that the *tuning in* is the perfecting of the listening technique and of meditation.

It is incorrect to think that the outer you is separate and apart from the *inner you*. Think of the outer and inner you as one. Try to think, feel, and act from the innermost center of being, from the Higher Mind (the kingdom of God within you); for here is the true center of your life and creative intelligence. This is the goal. Such an objective may appear distant and difficult, but as you go forward in your quest you will be sustained by an ever increasing sense of at-one-ment with the *inner you*, and your own unique kind of creativity will begin to manifest in your daily life.

Try to *tune in* every possible moment of the day to this inner you. This is the way of true prayer. When you reach a state of constancy in this, you will have begun to fulfill the command, "Pray without ceasing." True prayer is inner attunement with the God within, and has nothing to do with long and wordy supplications for things needed or unneeded; nor with those even more amazing discourses in which God is told what is going on in the world and what He should do about it.

Let the God within (Higher Self) become the center of your life, the home base through which you function and are most truly yourself. Higher Mind, the personality complex, and subconscious levels of awareness must live in unison, in oneness. They need to be aligned into a working, functioning whole. This is what is meant by the word, "holy," or holiness. Holiness is not piousness. It is not real or pretended goodness, nor any effort to be set apart from the whole of mankind. It refers to the complete, the whole and fully functioning unity of being. When this is attained then it may truly be said, "In Him we live and move and have our being."

You can enter the world of understanding, wisdom, and creativity by centering awareness upon that which is only to be found within—"for behold, the kingdom of God is within you." Seek it first and find it. Then you will never be alone or lonely again. Then there can be for you only infinite good, and the will and power to do the good that now you dream of in a wishful way. Then will wishing cease, and you will become a co-creator with God, a moving force for constructive good in a world whose need for this is very great.

Higher Mind is truly the pathway to creativity, and each one has access to this source of divine potential. Why then, you may ask, is it difficult to maintain conscious rapport with Higher Mind at the personality level? As has been pointed out, improper thought and emotion has created strong barriers which can only be removed by changing and refining these channels. This will act to remove the static generated by the personality, and will allow finer vibrations to enter the field of consciousness.

Look for guidance to the highest level of awareness you can reach. Then the channel between higher and lower mind will widen and deepen. If you would succeed, it is important to think beyond the personal self and reach out in love toward the Great Self of all.

CHAPTER 8

All Are Sons of God

It is not correct to assume that Higher Self is so much involved with its own superior levels of functioning that it has little interest in its personality, the outer you. The personality was brought into being by the God within to further and deepen awareness of the objective world. Only as the Higher Self is able to function through the personality can it fulfill this purpose. In one sense, also, the personality is a limitation which the Self has imposed upon the totality of being. This is a crucifixion upon "the cross of matter" which the Spiritual Self undergoes when it limits and confines a part of itself in a body of flesh.

However, there is expansion of consciousness and fulfillment for the Higher Self when the personality finally reaches the point where it can attain conscious at-one-ment with the God within and goes on to final liberation, symbolized in many of the great religions as mystical crucifixion and resurrection. The final act in the drama is the "ascension into Heaven." All are sons of God, and as such all can, in time, attain "unto the measure of the stature of the fulness of Christ."[1]

At this point, redeemed or liberated man becomes one with the inner god. There is no further need for incarnating in the personality and body of man, unless he chooses to do so for the purpose of helping those who remain behind. There are those who have done this and who, today, live on this planet. Although they have gone beyond the need of human, physical incarnation, they have chosen to help humanity in the long journey toward realization of true being. This path which we travel they know well, for they have gone along this selfsame way. They know the difficulties and hardships which will be encountered. Their compassion and love have caused them to turn their faces from rewards which they might have in other, more perfect, worlds. Their work is on inner levels of awareness. They form a great and dedicated brotherhood.

This brotherhood has need for new recruits for its band of servers, men and women who will be liaisons between their world and the world of men. Members of the brotherhood work in harmony with the periodic laws of nature and cannot go beyond those laws. They give help to those who want their help and who make an effort toward self-help. Each one must first do his utmost to help himself. He must understand, also, that when he receives help he must give aid to others. To take and give nothing can be likened to the story in which a man met a fairy and asked her for a gift of gold. The fairy said he could have all the gold his hat would hold. The fairy began to pour gold into the man's hat, but warned him to stop her before any overflowed and spilled upon the ground. The man was greedy and wished to make sure he received as much as possible. He did not stop the fairy in time. Suddenly, some of the gold spilled upon the ground. Sadly, the

---

[1] Eph. 4:13

man saw that the gold in his hat had turned to sand and the fairy was gone.

It is even so today: men ask for and receive treasures of spiritual gold, but if they take, and take, and never share with others, the treasures so freely given to them disappear. In other words, they lose the understanding that once they had.

Should you desire to become one of this band of servers the way is open. Especially, during the last quarter of each century is this true. Although the need is great, some important preparations are required. In this book are a few hints and suggested exercises that can start you on the way.

Contact with Higher Mind is important. This should not prove to be too difficult if you begin to clear away mental and emotional static and learn to *re-form* your thinking. Complete dedication and an ever-increasing selflessness are also important. Selflessness is not to be reached in one lifetime but much can be accomplished. And to light the way, there is the inner joy and peace of a tranquil mind.

Cultivate the Garden of Self

Should you desire to become one of the band of servers, and if you have the determination to do so, cultivate the garden of self, for outer self can well be compared to a garden. With the help of the *inner you* or Higher Self, it can be your privilege to make this garden of self into a place of beauty and loveliness.

When a weed first appears in a garden it is so small and fragile that it seems harmless. It could then be easily removed. But if allowed to remain, it soon will grow into a strong, sturdy plant, and its roots will penetrate deeply into the earth. Then much greater effort is needed to remove it. The same is also true in the garden of the personal self.

Weeds of selfishness, intolerance, and pride may become deeply imbedded but remain hidden from conscious awareness. They are like weeds which propagate not only from seeds but from underground runners, from which new plants spring up in profusion. If a small piece of such a root remains in the soil, it soon renews itself and again brings forth a crop of weeds.

Remove all traits of character, all action, thought, and emotion that can hinder true understanding for these are weeds which can destroy your potentially beautiful garden. Critical thoughts of others, also, are weeds that can become rank if allowed to grow and flourish. Daily examination of thoughts, feelings, and actions will prevent many imperfections from taking root in your character. Therefore, it is essential to discover the hidden roots (causes) of everything found in the garden of the personal self. All weeds must be uprooted, not just cut off, so that they will not reappear in months, years, or even lives hence. In the garden of self, uplifting emotions, proper thought, and right action are flowers to be cultivated and brought to full and glorious blossoming.

Today, chemicals are available that will kill weeds, both roots and outer plant; for those who would cultivate the garden of self there is also such a destroyer. It is love, and there are no bad side effects, which is not always so with weed-destroying chemicals.

If, in the garden of self, you cultivate such virtues as love, gentleness, kindness, patience, and reverence for life, then the center of love and power, which is the true you, will draw into itself ever finer and finer matter, casting out the coarser matter which alone can give life to gross thoughts and feelings. This finer matter will build up the personal force field into a finer and more responsive and more useful instrument.

Do not be disturbed or dismayed because of imperfections which you may uncover in the personal self.

This is to be welcomed, for it offers the opportunity to discover what is needed for further progress. Constant care and awareness are essential. However, this will not be a joyless task. You really are not giving up anything worth keeping. The old garments (habit patterns of thought and emotion) which have been designed and fashioned over a period of many lives have long since lost their usefulness. Now, you are ready to make for yourself new garments of great beauty.

Discovery of rigidity or even of ugliness in the personality should not arouse feelings of guilt or shame, or cause one to feel unworthy. Acknowledge such insight and understanding with gratitude, for until there is awareness nothing can be done to change for the better.

Virtues are to be valued and strengthened, but they should not be viewed with emotional attachment. Pride in one's virtues is easy to acquire and difficult to overcome. Virtues have been developed through effort —often through very great effort. Pride in having achieved a difficult goal is a common human feeling. One may not be aware that there is pride in a virtue. Therefore, examine well any virtues which you may recognize in yourself and try to determine if you have any feelings of superiority because of them. In particular, note how you feel about other individuals who do not have these virtues. Do you feel of superior quality or worth, or more worthy of honor or appreciation because of your virtues? It is necessary to remain unattached and dispassionate toward the virtues acquired, whatever they may be.

PART THREE:
STEPS ON THE PATHWAY

Look within your own mind—your personal field of awareness—for understanding. It awaits your examination. The search will be fruitful. Regularity or lack of regularity is the difference between success and failure. If you continue your search you will find the way to the Innermost Self, and when you succeed in making this contact you will know the truth—that life is a unity. (p. 71)

CHAPTER 9

Meditation

The (inner) you is truly the essence and wisdom of "that of god" which is within each and every one—not just the well-educated, the rich and powerful, the mentally gifted, or the wellborn. The technique of asking questions and of then stilling the mind by listening for answers is a method which I have found helpful. Others, who have tried it, say that the listening method appeals in two ways. First, it does not require months or years of practice to gain the needed skill for effective use. Second, one has available an ever-present source of guidance, of wisdom, and of creativity. This is not to say that all this can be achieved without dedicated effort and right motives. If your motives are to gain personal power, or if you hope to achieve psychic development which will enable you to impress or control others, even for their own good, then stop and reconsider. This is not for you. Your efforts will end in failure. Motivation must stem from the need to know the true, inner you, the God within, and through this knowing to express through thought and action an ever increasing harmony and perfection in your life.

This technique of asking questions and listening is only *one* method of approaching the *inner you* through contact with Higher Mind. There are many pathways, and each one must find his own path to the Innermost Self (the inner Christ). But by whatever name the *inner you* is called or by whatever path you may choose to travel, you will find a welcome home, even as the Prodigal Son was welcomed to his father's house.

The listening technique in itself does not take the place of meditation, which has long been the traditional way of communication with the intuitive level of mind. Many have testified to its importance in reaching such contact. I have found most effective for myself the combination of meditation, followed by listening for answers to questions. Before asking questions, some might like to use a short prayer or a favorite mantra. The important thing is to lift consciousness above the level of the outer, concrete mind to a higher or inner level of inspiration and intuitive awareness.

If there is sincere desire to contact the spiritual center of innermost being, the effort will be made to learn to meditate effectively, for this is of great value. I shall make no attempt to explore in-depth methods and techniques of meditation; excellent books are already available on this subject. The most difficult thing about meditation is to establish the habit of daily practice, preferably at a certain time each day. Regularity helps to establish such a daily habit, which is a problem for almost every beginning meditator. So many trivial and not-so-trivial involvements infringe on the time we may try to give to meditation that the temptation is often to skip it altogether. Despite the sea of confusion surrounding the average man or woman, there must be a driving determination to allot a certain time each day for communication with the God within: this is the first obligation. Indeed, this is the true meaning of the Biblical commandment, "Thou shalt have no other gods before me." Time and devotion lavished upon unessential externals are of no permanent value, but the time given to contemplation and meditation is of transcendent value.

When a desirable habit is well established, take care that it is maintained. Consider the man who overcomes a habit such as smoking. Just to prove that he has really conquered the habit, he decides to smoke one more time. To his dismay he finds that the new habit of not smoking was less firmly fixed than he had thought and that his previous smoking habit has returned in full force.

One must take care not to fall into old habits which, like some grim specter of the past, sit silently in wait until the newly formed habit is neglected or put aside for just this *one* time. Then, little by little, exceptions occur. There are always *logical reasons* for such exceptions. There is a pressing business or social engagement, lack of sleep or physical inertia—reasons are plentiful and endless.*

Some profess the desire to meditate but complain that they are unable to do so because of the many disturbances which interfere. He who waits for an ideal environment for meditation or for the perfect moment of inspiration waits in vain. The perfect moment never comes, and few environments approach the ideal. Distractions of many kinds are imposed by family and community situations.

The kingdom of peace and tranquility is not to be gained except through constant vigilance. On the pathway to this kingdom, there are mountains of discouragement to climb, stumbling blocks of indecision and distraction to overcome. Only the sword of the spiritual

---

* Meditation when sleepy is not recommended.

will can slay the enemies which will be met along the way. Only the pure in mind and heart can find at last the gateway through which the aspirant must enter.

Meditation can be likened to the tuning of a piano. If the piano is out of tune you get plenty of sound when the keys are struck, but there is little music. The sounds produced are not pleasing to hear. So it is with a personality that is not tuned in harmony with the inner God. A lifetime may be spent in many kinds of frantic activity, but little is accomplished in useful work. Such a life might well be compared to listening to music played upon an instrument badly out of tune. Instead of music there is only the noise of discordant sound.

The personality needs to be tuned through daily meditation into an instrument that can bring forth pure, clear, harmonious tones. Only then can the personality consciousness unite with the inner God and begin to produce beautiful music.

Such self-training, faithfully observed and perfected, is regenerative in effect. The force fields are acted upon and rearranged in orderliness and harmony—a harmony patterned upon the universal harmony. Unity of being will become established, so that the inner and outer man can act as a unit. The *inner you* does the rearranging with the cooperation and help of the outer you. This, then, is the true purpose of meditation, to achieve an inner wholeness and harmony.

A further thought on the purpose of meditation is to be found in *Meditation, a Practical Study,* by Adelaide Gardner (p. 62). She says:

Thus the purpose of meditation is at least two-fold. It is used to awaken the intuitional activities of the mental life, to make habitual thinking more illumined, more truthful than hitherto. At the same time it cultivates qualities that nurture and express the spiritual man. Further, the change in mental habit may lead to an intuitive approach to all problems and the growth of insight and serenity can, in time, establish an open line of communication between the waking consciousness and the spiritual source. . . .

Preliminary to effective meditation, it is necessary to learn to focus the mind and hold it steadily upon an idea, an object, a scene, or perhaps a mantra, for a definite time, whether this be for one or for twenty minutes. For the beginner, the time may be quite brief. It is not an easy task to hold the mind one-pointedly upon such an object or idea and sustain mental stillness for even a few minutes. This is particularly true if the attention is directed to something which has no personal interest or appeal. One may start by using a single, simple thing like a leaf, a pencil, or even a sheet of blank paper. Such an exercise helps in gaining conscious control of the mind, which like an unruly child, has been engaged in a constant frenzy of random activity. Now, the child of mind must learn to obey, and must modify its stream of activity into a more orderly and effective pattern of behavior.

If the mind is fixed upon an object of personal interest, the task may be less difficult than if focused upon an object that has no appeal. But if the attention is centered upon something totally lacking in interest for a period of two or more minutes without wavering, it will be an accomplishment of real value in the training of the mind. If, on subsequent days, the same object can be held in unwavering focus for a somewhat longer time, one can assume that significant progress is taking place. However, do not expect swift, day-by-day improvement in this ability to learn to narrow the field of mental focus and hold it free from intruding thoughts.[1]

---

[1] A valuable book with many exercises useful in training the mind is *Concentration, an Approach to Meditation* by Ernest Wood; Wheaton: Theosophical Publishing House, a Quest Book, 1967.

Let us assume that you want to begin meditation but because of other obligations and duties can allot to the practice only thirty minutes each day. You can accomplish much in a meditation period of fifteen or twenty minutes. More can be accomplished in one or two 15-minute periods of daily meditation than in longer meditations of the "off and on" variety, that is meditating for a few days or a week and then skipping a few days. Such random effort is far less helpful than shorter meditations faithfully performed each day.

Each individual must decide just how and when the allotted time is used, depending upon his own life situation. A 15-minute meditation once or twice daily should prove to be sufficient for the beginner. If meditation is a total mystery to you, for little more than one dollar you can purchase Adelaide Gardner's small but excellent book on meditation, previously referred to in this chapter.[2]

Of great value for the beginner, as well as for those who have meditated for years, is to spend five or ten minutes in the morning preparing oneself for the day. Start with a few deep, rhythmic breaths, which are helpful both for health and for relaxation. Then visualize yourself going through the entire day in such a way as to exemplify in thought and action the true *inner you*. For example, see yourself as being friendly and considerate toward those with whom you work, or visualize yourself expressing to members of your family the love and gentleness you would want to show them were this to be your last day with them. Consider such small but significant things as your tone of voice, even a pleasant look on your face and, above all, tell yourself that you will at all times maintain an inner feeling of peace and harmony. The maintenance of personal

---

[2] *Meditation, a Practical Study* by Adelaide Gardner; Wheaton Theosophical Publishing House, a Quest Book, 1973.

peace and harmony is a contribution each one can make toward the purification of the world's ecology— the ecology of the great mental and emotional atmosphere in which we live and move and have our being. Use your power of visualization to see yourself thinking, feeling, and acting in ways which will help to make the day as perfect as possible. In such small significant ways you can begin to be a co-creator with the *inner you,* the Spiritual Self, in reforming the thought, feeling, and action patterns of the outer you.

If you would undertake the retraining and reforming of the personal self through meditation, self-discipline, and contact with the *inner you,* do not overlook the need for strengthening essential qualities of character. They are the highly extolled but too often unused or out-of-fashion virtues, which have long been recommended and exemplified by the world's renowned saints, religious teachers, and philosophers, and by the great and noble of the many races of mankind. I refer to such well-known virtues as truthfulness, gentleness, graciousness, humor, joyousness, and love. The list can be lengthened or shortened to fit one's personal need. A helpful procedure is to enter in your notebook the virtues upon which you wish to work for a year. Devote a few minutes each day to consideration of one of the virtues. Visualize yourself expressing this quality in daily life in every possible way. Then ask the *inner you* to help you make this virtue an integral part of the outer you. And don't forget to ask for a little help in remaining free from self-pride in the achievement of these virtues. Spend a week or a month on each quality and then go on to the next virtue on your list until all have been covered. At that point you can start over again or add other needed virtues to your list.

This exercise could be part of the daily morning preparation for your day, or it could be an evening or noontime exercise. Progress notes can be entered in your notebook from time to time. Do not be discouraged if some time elapses before you can determine whether any real progress has been made.

The two suggested exercises for starting the day should take about ten minutes, and could be followed by a short meditation, say ten or fifteen minutes. If you find yourself wondering what to meditate for or about, you might be interested in a daily meditation for peace, harmony, right thought and right action. Such a meditation should not be directed toward all the world, but toward your community or city, and/or your family. The power generated by one person's meditation (and meditation is a source of power) would be spread too thin if directed toward all the people of the world. Such a meditation as this offers the opportunity to be a channel of blessing for family and community, and can help bring into actuality some measure of peace, harmony, right thought, and right action, all greatly needed in our time.

Sit in an upright position when meditating. Do not use a chair that invites slumping. Aim for comfort without tension, but keep mentally alert and awake. Take a few deep, slow, rhythmical breaths preliminary to starting meditation.

Directions for Peace Meditation

This meditation can be done in two ways. You can start by chanting the words *peace, harmony, right thought,* and *right action,* using the tones of *A* and *F* of the musical scale in the chanting. Or if you prefer, you can chant the notes *A* and *F* several times aloud, and as you chant listen inwardly to the tones. Then repeat softly, or mentally, say and think *peace, harmony, right thought* and *right action.* Then say softly or inwardly think, "Let there be peace, harmony, right thought and right action in this home and in this community and the surrounding area. In the homes, the schools, the churches, the places of business—wherever men, women, and children meet to work, or play, or study, let there be peace, harmony, right thought, and right action. May I be a channel for Thy peace. Peace, peace, peace." (The *Thy* used here refers to the inner Christ.) After this, just *be*. That is, maintain a feeling of peace and harmony, but be as mentally still as possible and let the *inner you* do the work.

The words can be used as given or changed in any way you wish to make the meditation more meaningful to you.

This peace meditation can also be used at any time during the day or in the evening. It can be used as the basis for group meditation. If such a group meets once each week for meditation, individual group members can do much good by using the meditation daily as an individual effort, but if possible each of the group members meditating at the same time each day or evening. This would continue the group effect, which gives much added power beyond the number of individuals involved.

You might wonder why the tones are used. This need not seem strange if you recall that sound through the media of vocal and instrumental music has long been used to help build the proper atmosphere for worship in most churches and temples. These tones act to clear away mental and emotional static. The note *A* is said to be the sound to use for *peace*. (This information came through inspirational *listening* by a member of the meditation group mentioned earlier in this book.) In any event, use of the tones seems to be effective in lifting consciousness in preparation for meditation.

Many in the world today are meditating for peace and harmony, and when the majority of the world's population are doing this, and living it, then will peace come as a reality in our world. Those who wish to further this work may do so by joining in this meditation for the renewal and purification of the world's mental and emotional atmosphere.

We have heard much about the pollution of the earth's air, water, and soil. The ecology of our world extends far beyond such boundaries. It embraces, also, the great and all-enveloping oceans of thought and feeling. We can start at once to renew and make clean these great reservoirs of polluted mental and emotional matter which completely surround us. No new bond issue will be needed, nor will any extra taxes be required to begin to clean up the mental and emotional pollution which has made the entire world population a sick and ailing people.

Meditation as a Source of Energy

Meditation should not be engaged in as a dreary but necessary exercise to be accomplished and have done with for the day. Such an attitude may have something useful to contribute to the inner growth and character of the man or woman who meditates in this way, but what a waste of potential when there is so much more that meditation can do! Meditation can renew the life force and creative energy and bring them into manifestation through the physical, mental, and emotional components of our being. There is a sense of joyous wholeness, of heightened awareness of the constantly changing but living miracle of all creation.

The creative artist, musician, or poet deeply involved in his work frequently enters a deeply meditative state. Great composers, inventors, sculptors, and other creative workers have testified to this through their letters or journals. Some have clearly told of the steps taken to reach the goal of creative achievement. Walter Russell, American musician, writer, painter, architect, and sculptor, in this century has confirmed the importance of meditation in attaining a high level of creativity. At the age of fifty-six, without having had any training in sculpture, Russell did a portrait bust of Edison which was acclaimed widely.

At that time Walter Russell was president of the Society of Arts and Sciences, which was to present a medal to Edison, but the artist who was to have done the work failed in his assignment. It was then that Russell decided to do the portrait bust himself to demonstrate his "inspired belief" in the power of man to work in unity with the "Universal One." He says:

> So I went to Florida with a mass of clay, but on my way down I spent the entire time absorbed in inspirational meditation with the Universal Source of all inspiration, in order to fully realize the omnipotence of the Self within me as a preparation for doing in a masterly way what I would otherwise be unable to do.[3]

Walter Russell went on to do many things in the medium of sculpture, including a monument of Mark Twain with twenty-eight figures, although he had never done a monument before. It too was a magnificent success.

It takes a very special kind of dedication and self-discipline to achieve such creative feats. Few will try to duplicate them, but there are many who would like to begin to live a more creative and more joyous life. For these, meditation can point the way.

---

[3] *The Man Who Tapped the Secrets of the Universe* by Glenn Clark, p. 19.

The Use of Mantras in Meditation

Much attention has been given in recent years to the use of mantras in meditation. This has great appeal for many. Mantras can aid in focusing the mind and lifting consciousness to an inner and more intuitive level. A mantra may be a single syllable, or it can be a short verse or phrase. Musical notes, also, can be used as mantras as in the peace meditation already noted.

If you would like to use a mantra when meditating, the three below offer a choice, or others that appeal to you, of course, may be used:

1. God is perfect life. I am one with God, therefore, I am whole and perfect in all my being and parts. God's healing forces are all about. I am well and at one with the God within.

2. God is perfect love. I am one with God. We are one and the same. God speaks through love. I act through God's love. Therefore, I am love.

3. More radiant than the sun, subtler than the ether is the Self, the Spirit within my heart, I am that Self, that Self am I.

Repeat the chosen mantra. Think about it and emotionally react to it. Try to feel yourself as one with the inner God, or Spiritual Self. If you prefer, you can think of yourself as one with the Christ Consciousness. If you feel that you should not claim, "I am one with God. We are one and the same," recall that in the Holy Bible it is written, "I have said, Ye are gods; and all of you are children of the Most High."[4]

After you have said the mantra and reacted to it, just *be*. Hopefully, you will have reached a state of comparative inner stillness and will be unconcerned as to whether you think or do not think. In this time of still-

_____
[4] Ps. 82:6

ness, the higher or *inner you* will know exactly what to do for your inner perfecting and outer and inner growth. Be still and trust in the God within.

CHAPTER 10

Self-Understanding

If you would follow the path which leads to creativity and inner unfoldment, self-understanding must be pursued every step of the way. This is of first importance and is not to be gained in a few easy lessons. The understanding which is needed must go deeper than the surface of personality. It is necessary to become increasingly aware of why one feels, thinks, and acts as one does. This requires insight into motives. Little progress can be made until there is more than superficial discernment. For this you will require all the resources at your command. At personality level, practice self-observation of habit and reaction patterns. Try to be as impersonal as if you were looking at an acquaintance or a child you hoped to understand.

When anger, fear, irritation, or a sense of guilt arises, it is important to understand the feeling and to try to discover its hidden as well as its known causes. Projecting personal bias and wrong action upon others will only compound the problems and create new stumbling blocks. Motives, often, are deeply hidden from conscious awareness.

To track down such unconscious motives and to be able to deal with them constructively without emotional trauma, you will need, also, the wisdom and aid of Higher Mind. For this the technique of inner listening (already explained) can prove to be a direct and useful approach. It is important to keep written records of all that takes place. If you will consistently carry out such a program, much self-knowledge can be gained.

Look within your own mind—your personal field of awareness—for understanding. It awaits your examination. The search will be fruitful. Regularity or lack of regularity is the difference between success and failure. If you continue your search you will find the way to the Innermost Self, and when you succeed in making this contact you will know the truth—that life is a unity. Then you will understand why devotion to the cause of humanity and of all life is the key which unlocks the door of the Temple of Wisdom. You cannot serve life if only the personal self is of importance to you, for this is a denial of the basic unity of being.

When you ask for understanding and guidance from Higher Self, help is given, but there is a condition for its continuance. As you gain understanding, it is necessary that you, also, become a channel for helping others. But if the help you offer is rejected, do not, because of this, waste time and energy in emotional reactions, for this is a subtle form of selfishness and springs from desire for personal appreciation.

Rejection has often been the lot of those who dedicate their lives to the cause of humanity and its betterment. Happily, you will meet a few along the way who will welcome help and who will begin to travel the path which leads to liberation from the bondage of the personal self.

Be aware of the hidden dangers that lurk in the voluminous robes of selfishness, whose cloud-like murkiness pervades the world. This is so much a part of the fabric of man's life that he is not even aware of it. Indeed, some forms of selfishness are considered virtues worthy of praise, to be extolled and rewarded. Be aware of this danger if you would walk the path toward self-understanding and enlightenment.

Seek for the inner light which alone can reveal the gossamer folds of selfishness which bind men in a prison of their own making. The fly caught in the spider's web finds that it is unable to extricate itself, even though the web appears a fragile, almost nonmaterial thing. So also do men become enmeshed in the all but invisible net of selfishness, which is stronger than bands of steel. See that you touch not with exploratory fingers of desire the web of selfishness that permeates the world about you.

The light within, even though small, is powerful and will deeply penetrate and reveal the many intertwining threads of selfishness which are everywhere present. These may appear to be as innocent as a mist of dew upon a rose petal, but look with the inner eye and the hidden dangers will be revealed.

Walk upon the path toward enlightenment with the sure knowledge that you need not walk alone and in darkness. The Spiritual Self within is ever present and is able and willing to guide you and provide the aid you need.

"Ask and you shall receive," is not a vain promise. It is a reality in Nature, itself. Trust in this good law. Believe in this promise and so shall you walk toward the mountain heights of the Spirit, even unto the sanctuary of the Most High.

Self-understanding is not reached by hiding from personal awareness problems that should be confronted and recognized. Self-deception can bring neither understanding nor progress. If in your quest for self-knowledge you discover that your character is less admirable than you had assumed it to be, do not be disturbed. Continue to observe the outer you as objectively as you can. If what you see displeases you there is no need for feelings of guilt or self-dislike. However, if your self-evaluation reveals many excellent qualities of character, with outstanding emotional stability, there is also no cause for pride or self-praise. This is only another form of self-deception.

Know that good and evil are not terms of exact and unchanging meaning. The primitive may be honored for killing his enemy and displaying his victim's shrunken head as an ornament attesting his prowess and bravery. Among some tribes this gives the warrior in his world the honor that wealth, business success, or political achievement gives to a man in the western world. Ethical standards can be of a social or tribal nature; not all are based upon eternal verities, universal in application.

When you recognize easily in another a weakness or fault, look also within yourself for the same weakness, hidden from self-awareness. Do not shrink from bringing forth from the depth of memory's storehouse those things which are covered over and wrapped in layer upon layer of illusion.

In your zeal for discovering and uprooting undesirable habits, thoughts, emotions, or actions, take care that you do not spend your time in constantly thinking about errors and mistakes. This is not helpful. The important thing is to recognize and observe these with as much detachment as possible, and then determine wherein a change for the better can be made. Progress can be achieved far more easily by spending time each day contemplating this more worthy ideal self-picture. Life is a living, growing thing and does not stand still. This is as true at the human level as it is at other levels. You can go forward toward your highest ideals by keeping the goal before you and by steadily pressing on in thought and action toward fulfillment.

If, however, you continually think upon times of weakness and failure, the positive forces for advancement are negated. Instead of progress the individual may actually repeat old mistakes and become like the "backsliding sinner," who is constantly repenting sins he is doomed to repeat. By dwelling upon past mistakes, one creates powerful thought forms of a negative or destructive kind that are attached to him, ready-made as it were, to influence his future. This is why many individuals fail to achieve those good and noble intentions which they glimpse within themselves in moments of inspiration and hopefulness. Instead of contemplating the goal to be reached, they allow the mind to dwell upon past errors. At best, this can only make for very slow progress. Much more can be accomplished by thinking of the desired goal and of ways and means of implementing the positive good to which you aspire. In this way, while one's own errors should be recognized and accepted, their energies can be transmuted into positive strength for the greater task.

Visualize yourself as living according to the highest principles known to you. The goal for man is not downward into the depths of matter and sensation, but forward and upward toward enlightenment. Joy and tranquillity of mind and spirit are the rewards that come from such a course of thought and action.

Success is best assured if one does not fasten upon a virtue and push it too hard. That is a path which leads to rigidity. Let there be constancy in your effort, but a little *give* is also to be desired. This is the needed elasticity required. But be aware, also, that there can be too much *give*. Seek for harmony and balance. Remember always that you are sons and daughters of the most high Spiritual Self.

CHAPTER 11

Elasticity is Needed

Consider the matter of elasticity and how a lack of
this can be a hindrance in the development of an integrated and harmonious wholeness of mind and spirit.
The emotional and mental "set" of the personality
might be likened to a rubber band. Originally, this
pure, strong rubber band had great strength and elasticity. New ideas and thoughts could pull and stretch
the band of mind and emotion and the *stress* could be
taken with ease. But as time passed, the effects of environment altered and changed this initial resilience. Rigidity of thought in certain *emotionally colored* concepts began to take the stretch out of what once could
give but still return to its original form.

Now, when rubber is subjected to stress it loses its
elasticity and starts to disintegrate; and when this takes
place it cannot be restored. Fortunately for man, the
rubber band of mind and emotion can be renewed, and
will again have life and "stretch." However, this is not
easily accomplished. It can be achieved only through

much effort, through understanding of the problems involved, and through the help of higher levels of mind or consciousness. This, in part, explains why it is important to practice self-examination of motives, actions, and patterns of thought.

To think, act, and feel according to a pattern makes it less difficult to adjust to the stress and strain of a particular environment or social group. Such acceptance of group *mores* is commonly thought of as *culture*. We have been cultured to fit into a mold of thinking and of behavior acceptable to our social, religious, and political groups. Such culture patterns tend to be rigidly frozen far into the future, beyond any valid necessity, although their roots may be found in past needs.

In our world today are many cultures with fixed patterns of belief and action which belong in this category. We have numerous cultures and subcultures, and many members of these groups tenaciously hold fast to old prototypes and spend much time and thought justifying and defending their desirability and usefulness. Powerful forces often are used to compel individuals to conform to established patterns and rituals. This can take the form of ridicule or social ostracism as well as many other kinds of disapproval and punishment.

In the past, when each small or large culture group was living apart from other groups, often separated by barriers of distance too great to be easily surmounted, problems that arose from cultural differences were not of world-shaking significance. But in today's world many of these problems have become tremendously important. Distance has ceased to be the barrier it once was.

Can you not see the dangers which confront us because of this? On this planet is a vast population, all members of many cultures and subcultures, caught in rigid molds of behavior, thought, and action patterns, which at some more or less remote point in time may have served important needs for group survival and harmonious existence. However, in our rapidly changing world this rigid culture heritage can bring dissension, violence, and conflict.

This is a world situation which cannot be quickly remedied. Always, there is great resistance to change. Established religious, political, social, and educational institutions are the entrenched guardians of our cultural heritage, and are committed to maintaining the status quo. Despite this commitment, widespread dissatisfaction, unrest, and violence threaten to overthrow or greatly alter and change some of our oldest and most sacred institutions. Technology and science in many ways have transformed the world environment in dramatic fashion. This is bringing about some experimental and sometimes bizarre changes.

Who could have envisioned, at the onset of the twentieth century, that before its end technological and scientific advances would develop so rapidly, or bring into daily use such things as radio, television, and airplanes that travel faster than sound? Who could have imagined that by the middle of the century atomic power would be used for the production of bombs which could in seconds destroy an island or a great city? And who would have dreamed that in this same century men would make aerial journeys to the moon and walk upon its surface?

These marvels of scientific technology have not resulted in the advent of the hoped-for millennium. Instead, violence and unrest are widespread. Declared and undeclared wars continue to destroy the lives of young and old and to lay waste cities and countryside. In so-called peaceful countries violence, also, flourishes. Many high school and college youths are in open rebellion against the established order. Numerous dissident groups are protesting volubly and sometimes with guns, fire, and looting. It would seem that the age of violence is upon us.

Dramatic changes in world environment have continued throughout this century, and at an accelerated pace. Even the Catholic Church, which in the religious world long stood like a rock, firm and unchanging, has made drastic changes. No longer is it required that the mass be chanted in Latin. Some members of the priesthood are working to change the requirement of the church that they be celibate, and scores have left the church to marry. Nuns, who formerly dressed in sober, medieval-styled robes, are now wearing clothes that do not set them apart significantly from other women. Even the holiness of the saints has been challenged, and numerous well-loved and honored saints have been abruptly removed from their sacred category. Many in the church, as well as in other areas of the total culture, still cling to the old ways. But prophetic of what may come in the future are the changes already made, and there is continued clamor for more and greater change. A prophet is not required to predict that further innovations are inevitable.

Often, it has been said that man's technology has outstripped his morality. This leaves him in a most vulnerable position. However true this may be, the question now is what can be done to lessen tension and violence and bring about peace and harmony?

The real hope for the world still remains as always the inner unfoldment and development of the individual man or woman. As this takes place in more and more members of the various cultures and subcultures, there is being built up a group of workers for the uplifting of the whole of mankind. Powerful thoughts for good can build a strong force field for the right kind of change—and change there must and will be. Let it be for the uplifting of mankind and not for his destruction and degradation!

Greatly needed in this time of cataclysmic change are men and women who will lift themselves out of lower levels of emotional and mental turmoil and stagnation into higher levels of awareness. Only then can one have the understanding which will enable him to be of real help in building a new and better world for all men.

CHAPTER 12

Your Spiritual Force

Good intentions and high aspirations are helpful. But you will need the force and power of will to transform these into action. Will, as here used, is not a kind of stubbornness but a spiritual force. It is an energy factor that can cut cleanly through physical inertia.

Through the powerful help of spiritual will the personality, with its physical body and strong desire nature, can be quickened into more vibrant life. The heavy, dull vibrations of the whole personality force field will be recharged with energy, and the coat of flesh and robe of desire will take on the radiance of bodily health and emotional purity. Then, and only then, can the light of Higher Mind penetrate the shadows and obstructions that previously seemed almost insurmountable. When this takes place there will be an expanding awareness and an increase in creative thought and action.

You ask, "How does one activate the force of spirit in the personal life?" The answer is: one starts by making use of the will which one now has. Whenever you determine to do a thing make sure to carry it through. This requires self-discipline, and is best and most easily achieved when the task undertaken is not too difficult for success. If doubt exists as to your ability to do a predetermined task, try to focus upon a small part of the whole project, and do that without fail. Then go on to another fractional part as often as necessary, until the whole of your objective has been accomplished in a series of easy stages. As you become stronger in the area of will, you can give yourself more difficult assignments with full expectation of success.

Ideally, training of the will should begin early in life and should continue throughout the entire life span. Training of the will is like physical exercise, of little value unless practiced with regularity.

Do not lose sight of the true meaning of *will*. It arises from the highest source of Being and is a quality of the spiritual or Higher Self. The strength and force of the will, when fully developed, are beyond the power to imagine. Let no day pass that you do not strengthen this aspect of yourself.

Do not expect immediate and dramatic results. The strengthening of the will may come about slowly and for a time any progress may be imperceptible to you. Only after some time has elapsed will you be able to look back and see that significant gains have been made.

Set your immediate goal, for this or any other area of self-training that you undertake, no higher than you can through effort succeed in attaining. Do not try to grasp the stars in one desperate reach. Rather, reach out one arm's length at a time and advance step by step, and as you go forward reach ever toward the perfection you seek, little by little. Let there be no impatience in your seeking. Relax, enjoy each moment, and know the joy and peace that can be an integral part of every moment of every day.

CHAPTER 13

Love Can Hasten Progress

In answer to a question concerning the possibility of speeding up progress I received this answer:

"There is a way. It is through love. Love is a force and a power of monumental strength. It resides in the innermost being of all men, but for many it remains deeply hidden and rarely is glimpsed or realized. It has been truly said that God is love. If you could understand what love is you would understand what God is. Love is that force in man that moves to every good and true action.

"Many things are labeled with the name of love, but love is not always to be found in the strange anomalies that are sometimes called by that name. In the name of love crimes have been committed against love. And ofttimes in the name of love selfishness has been enthroned.

"The emotion called love is but a shadow without substance when compared with the reality of love. Love is the seed and root of life. Meditate upon love

82

that the true meaning of its nature may be revealed to you, and that love may be as a lamp shining within you to light your way to inner knowledge and true understanding."

Then I asked, "How shall I go about this?"

The answering thoughts which came were these:

"Think upon love. After you have considered it in as many ways as you can, try to realize that you are love. Then cease to think, and just *be love*. If you meditate upon love in this way day after day, there will come understanding and true awareness of the nature and power of love.

"Knock and the door will open. Try! And then try again! Do not expect a few faint knocks (efforts) to open the door to the Kingdom of Love, but every effort made will bring you a little closer to the ultimate goal. Remember, also, that right motives are important for success. Let not your thought be concerned with nor centered upon ultimate results. Relax and be at peace. Value each moment and know its joy, looking neither backward nor forward."

As I continued to meditate upon love and to ask for understanding, I began to be aware that love is not something that words can explain, but that it has to be realized. I was at that time spending regular daily periods meditating on love and listening for answers to my questions regarding it following the meditations.

Some of the answers received are given here as transcribed from my notebooks:

"Think not of love as an intellectual concept. Love is a force that must be turned on and used. Even as you cannot light your house by thinking of light, but must turn the switch to connect with the source of power, so must you do more than intellectualize about love, or try to feel pleasantly emotional about it.

"The nature and power of love is much misunderstood. Love can regenerate and renew. Without love life itself would have little meaning. Without love a child cannot survive in health of mind or body. For lack of love the old lose interest in living and even will to die.

"Do not underestimate the power of love. Even to scrub a floor with love is better for the floor and less tiring for you. To clean a house with love, as well as with hard work, will make the house cleaner and will fill it with thought forms of joy and blessing.

"Love acts as a catalyst to overcome inertia, which is the result of a lack of love in action. Let even the lowliest task be an expression of love. Remember that every animate and inanimate thing has been brought into being by the force of the Creator's loving thought. Each touch or contact you have with even an inanimate object, if love is there, can in some small way help to lift it toward its own 'greater selfhood.'

"Love the God within and love yourself, for then you can better understand what love is and what it can do. Love your children, your wife, your husband, your father, your mother, your brothers and sisters, and love your friends. Give love freely to all, and as you grow in understanding, the time will come when you will radiate love to all beings, to all life.

"Continue to meditate upon love and let your actions be a reflection of love. Proper action is love expressed through action. Then, indeed, does action become pleasant and its own reward."

Somewhat later this was recorded:

"Love is Being at its center of balance and power. Love creates, heals, and gives life. The Creator's love holds all things in balance and order.

"Let order and balance be an integral part of your daily life, for then the center of Self rests easily upon a pivot of strength, serene and free from strain or stress.

"Love is the cohesive force of the universe. It is creativity in action. It can bring harmony and peace into the world."

Through inner listening I was warned not to try to influence or change the opinions and actions of others, either directly or in subtle and devious ways. Apparently, this came to me as the result of my having tried to influence certain members of my family whose beliefs and attitudes I considered harmful to them. I was somewhat appalled to discover that my long and faithful effort to influence and change people for their own good was really a disservice to them, with possible karmic involvement for me. The message which came to me follows:

"Only love and gentleness can awaken the outer personality to the God within. This is important to remember in your relationships with members of your family and with friends as well as with all others with whom you come in contact. In the name of love do not seek to wrap restraining bands around a loved one to control and mold the shape or pattern of his thought and action. Each individual must learn from his own life experiences and make his own decisions and then assume responsibility for them. This does not release from personal accountability those who try to change and influence others. There is an interplay of karma in such cases, and the interwoven threads of karma can, and indeed often do, reach far into the future, even unto many lives to come. Therefore, take great care in such matters.

"Even with children there is no need for overcontrol and undue restraint. An example of right action on the part of the would-be teacher or child guide is most important. A child needs to be given instruction and guidelines but he needs, also, freedom to think his own thoughts, to explore, and to test within safe limits."

CHAPTER 14

Creativity Has Many Faces

This book is almost finished. It can be read and put aside, or it can serve as a guide for the most rewarding journey you will ever make—a journey that will lead from the prison of the personal self to the undiscovered splendor of the Innermost Self.

To reach this goal there will be a time of preparation and growth. This period might be likened to the cycle of gestation preparatory for birth. Exercises and techniques for this growth-time have been clearly indicated, and the necessity for training and self-discipline has been purposely stressed, for this is of paramount importance.

The ideas presented for your consideration are predicated upon a foundation of reality rather than of belief. A few citations have been given of individuals who have found the way to creativity and accomplishment through contact with inner levels of mind. These are only a few of the many who have, through such contact, reached a high level of creativity in various fields of endeavor.

You can live a creative life even though you never paint a picture, write a poem, compose a musical symphony, or do original work in one of the scientific disciplines. The creative faculty is not limited to the arts, to science, invention, or any other field of activity. It can express itself in every aspect of life in many unique and personal ways. Each individual has a creative level of mind, and when contacted it can and does give dimensions of greatness to any work undertaken. It brings insight and understanding to every problem upon which it is brought to bear. If you would live a full and creative life, give this higher, intuitive part of yourself full authority to guide and direct your day by day activities, feelings, and thoughts. As this aspect of yourself takes over more completely you will discover that problems disappear and new and unforeseen opportunities and benefits result in personal good for you, as well as for others with whom you come in contact.

If you do not find yourself artistically gifted or even interested in the arts, or if you have no special affinity for science in its many far-flung fields, you can still be creative in your own way. The business man, the office worker, the farmer tilling the land and working with plants, all of these can work better and with greater personal joy if the creative Higher Mind is given control.

The teacher who can lift the awareness of his or her students, inspiring them to new heights of aspiration and effort, is a creative individual. Such a teacher can do much to raise the level of student achievement and may start many on the path which ultimately will lead to true creativity.

The mother who provides an atmosphere of warmth, peace, and love for her children, generating an environment that nurtures and expands their creative potential, is herself demonstrating a significant degree of creativity. A young mother who hoped some day to have time for creative work said: "When my children are older, perhaps I can go back to school and learn to do some creative thing. I am too busy now even to try." This mother made the mistake of equating creativity with accomplishment in the limited area of the arts.

A young man excused his failure to develop the natural talent he knew he had. "I think I could be creative," he remarked, "if I had money to go to school for the training I need. Without such training I can do nothing."

Now, the creative mind is ready and willing to help regardless of the gravity of the problem with which one is faced. The matter of attending a suitable school for needed training and the perplexities connected with the rearing and training of children are problems not beyond its capabilities. These and other difficulties can be resolved with the help of Higher Mind.

Listening to music can leave one untouched in any meaningful way, or it can be an experience that lifts consciousness into a higher dimension. To walk along the seashore and observe the profoundly moving beauty and inexplicable mysteries of nature may awaken the sleeping outer mind into a new and deeper awareness, or it can be no more than a walk along a sandy beach that happens to be near the ocean.

One can read a book creatively. Many read well and can quote accurately what they read. This demonstrates a good memory, but it is not creativity. If you can "tune in" to the consciousness of the author and translate this deeper understanding into something more personally meaningful, then you partake of another dimension of creativity.

Children sometimes show true creativity in solving play-time difficulties. An example of this was brought to my attention by a mother whose small daughter was involved. A group of young children were happily playing, but this soon gave way to arguing and fighting when they decided to play "families." All wanted to be parents. No one was willing to be a child. The mother, observing the group, was about to offer the suggestion that they take turns being parents, when a little four-year-old girl solved the problem and restored harmony within the group when she exclaimed, "Oh, let's all be orphans!" The children were delighted with this way of solving their dilemma. Here was a demonstration of child-wisdom that had a touch of mature genius.

Many individuals put aside all thought of trying to develop innate, creative potential because of the problems confronting them, and with which they grapple endlessly and all too often with hopeless futility. Today, our world is beset with problems clamoring to be solved. Indeed, there is desperate need for creativity in many areas of problem solving on every level of life, personal and public. Newspaper headlines and television broadcasts point up the more serious city, state, national, and world problems. There are also the personal problems which each one must recognize and try to solve. These could be resolved with greater dispatch and adequacy if approached with the insight and understanding of the creative, intuitive mind.

I recall times in my own life when I spent weary hours and even days trying to solve personal problems. The more I agonized, the larger and more devastating the difficulties appeared. Now, I realize that had I taken my problems to a higher level of consciousness for understanding and help there need not have been those times of vacillation and indecision. Such an emotional approach to any problem area generates mental and emotional static to such an extent that there is little possibility of reaching a creative level of mind.

Man's failure to attain his creative potential may be

and often is the result of two illusions which have widespread acceptance. The primary error starts with the premise that man *is* his physical body. This causes him to place undue emphasis upon everything which has to do with this aspect of himself. His constant concern for the body is rooted, essentially, in this belief. As a result of this misconception, the second illusion follows: it says that man's chief good is the enjoyment of pleasure. This results in the effort to gratify every physical and emotional desire. Thought and emotion constantly are channeled into these lower levels of awareness in the mistaken belief that through the gateway of physical and emotional gratification one can enter an enchanted land that will result in fulfillment and happiness.

This is the ancient philosophy of Hedonism which has ever promised its devotees happiness, but has never given them anything more substantial than the momentary pursuit of sensation. The hungry pilgrim is offered husks and chaff instead of the threshed and nourishing grain. Regardless of how the golden chaff glitters, it is like an insubstantial mirage which leads only to disappointment and hopelessness.

If on your journey of self-discovery you would awaken the creative potential which is your birthright, do not be misled into believing that you are the physical body and that your greatest good is to be found in the pursuit of pleasure.

Let the true *inner you* direct your course. Instead of circling round the mountain or taking off on some meandering bypath, you can go straight through to your goal. Regular, daily practice of meditation and *listening* are two powerful methods of quickening the inner life forces. The physical, emotional, and lower mental components of yourself will begin to be harmonized, refined, and rearranged into a more responsive, more perfect wholeness.

You may read these words and conclude that, possibly, there are available courses of study, lessons, or books which will offer easier and more magical methods of approaching transcendental levels of consciousness. It is true that there are to be had lessons and courses of study which claim to reveal profound and secret teachings which will give the student instant cosmic consciousness, or which offer him quick and easy access to psychic powers, which will enable him to control the minds and lives of others. If you could find such a course of study that would really do this, it would be wise to avoid it as if it were a black plague.

If you believe yourself to be in contact with Higher Mind and the intuitive level of awareness, observe the kind of teaching you receive. If it violates the time-honored ethical principles found in all great religions, you may be sure the information is not from higher levels of consciousness. Your own inner yardstick of conscience should be the measure by which you evaluate the authenticity of all you receive.

Some individuals value a thing only by the monetary price tag with which it is labeled. Such persons will be interested only in teachers or schools that charge high prices for the "truth" they dispense to their pupils. There are many such schools. For their lessons and courses of study, they find it more profitable to draw out to a fine thread the string of truth. The unsatisfied seeker continues to pay for months and years as he continues his fruitless search for the magical elixir of truth, which alas cannot be found in either books or lessons. These can offer only methods of approach. Truth comes through inner realization and knowing. To find this "pearl of great price" the pupil must enter the temple of higher consciousness through the gateway of self-discipline, persistence, and utter dedication to highest principles. His motives must be pure and, insofar as is possible, free from selfishness. There is no other way. But given these qualities, anyone can succeed.

Here before you the table has been spread with food for your use. But each one must, himself, eat and digest the food. If the table appears bare of delicacies and rich desserts, let the seeker search for them and bring them to his table. But let him not sit helplessly at the table and talk of the fine rich food he has found. Food spoken about or food spread upon the table will not nourish the body until it is eaten, digested, and assimilated. First, you must eat the food before it can sustain life.

CHAPTER 15

Reach For The Stars

Man seeks to understand the universe because he is a child of the universe and wants to know whence he came. Man wants to identify himself and know his place in the cosmos. As mankind we reach to the stars, not only because they are above us and, splendid in their grandeur, seem greater and more profound than we, but also because man has always sensed that the secrets of his origin lie therein. . . . Man continues to reach for the stars because his consciousness, his being, allows no other choice. He is driven, for surely the search for answers to the riddle of time cannot forever be thwarted.[1]

Even those who do not succeed in reaching superior heights of creative genius may take exploratory steps along the pathway of creativity. Each one who under-

---

[1] From a lecture, *The Wonders of Space*, by Capt. Edgar D. Mitchell at Hot Springs, Ark., May 28, 1972, in which he gave some personal reactions to his trip to the moon on Apollo 14.

takes these self-training techniques and faithfully continues to work may confidently expect to make measurable progress. Should you desire to become one of the truly creative individuals, be aware that requirements include not only high aspirations, but the ability to contact and enter the realm of Higher Mind, and then to follow through with action. This last requirement is of utmost importance.

It is the nature of Higher Mind to be creative, to express itself in what Plato termed archetypal ideas. Only the personality, through the use of lower mind and the vision of Higher Mind, can translate these symbolic idea-forms into tangible objectivity—objects of art, poems, musical compositions, etc. Even as flowers bless the world with their beauty, so does Higher Mind bless mankind with the gift of wisdom and creative thought and action. This gift is available to all who seek it.

Thoughts clothed in beautiful word-pictures which move across the canopy of mind cannot be retained and again brought forth unless captured and recorded. The time to do this is at the moment when consciousness is lifted on wings of inspiration beyond the level of the logical, reasoning mind. Do not wait until a more convenient moment, for then you may discover that you have at your command only the plodding lower mind whose very best efforts are far removed from creativity. Poets, artists, and musicians of past centuries, when attempting to reach the creative mind, spoke of it as "courting the Muse." Today, you might think of this as invoking Higher Mind. The meaning is one and the same.

In this century man has used his creative genius to accomplish technological miracles. The twentieth century has seen man reach for the stars and plant his feet and his machines upon the moon, more than 221,000 miles from the earth. In doing this man has traveled at a speed so great that had anyone at the beginning of this century suggested the possibility of such a feat, he would have been considered mad.

Now, we are at the threshold of a new century, and already we see that exploration of inner space has begun. Harbinger of greater things to come is the growing scientific interest in this exploration, but the world of mind still remains more of a mystery than that of the farthest stars. A few intrepid explorers have begun to point the way and are bringing into the realm of the possible some things that were thought to be forever locked in unfathomable mystery.

Will man now begin to look beneath the shallow surface of outer mind, that ten or fifteen percent he now uses, and discover the vast expanse that awaits him? The doorway is close at hand and available to all who are willing to make the effort to venture into this almost unknown realm. This exploration will not require great sums of gold or silver to pay for building intricate machines. Already, each one has all that is needed to begin his own private journey to inner space of mind.

Sophisticated machines and many trained and disciplined men were required for the journey to outer space, but for the journey into the inner space of mind no better or more perfect machine has been created than the physical-emotional-mental complexity called *man*. For man is uniquely equipped with all the necessary instruments to begin this journey of exploration. This man-machine has a built-in mechanism for self-correction of mistakes which is more efficient for its purpose than the present day wonder, the self-correcting computer.

Only the best could compete to become astronauts, and then began the arduous discipline and training which developed a crew capable of taking a rocket-fired vehicle to the moon. For the exploration of mind, every man, every woman, every teen-age boy and girl may begin his or her own private flight.

You begin where you now are. It is not required that you be one of the top two percent, the so-called mentally gifted. Wherever you may be on the psychologically-devised intelligence quotient scale is not really important here. Each one has an inner, Higher Mind, whose capacity for creativity and accomplishment is not bound by the prison of lower mind.

Self-discipline and training are just as essential for those who would travel to inner space of mind as they are for outer-space-bound astronauts. Training for inner space travel can be started at any time. Should you reach only an outpost comparable to the moon in your journey toward planets and stars, this still will be a great beginning. It matters not that today you may find yourself locked in the narrow confines of outer mind, but it is important to begin and then go steadily forward.

Exploration of outer space will take more than one generation to accomplish; so also, the journey to inner space of Higher Mind may not be fully achieved in one lifetime. Space exploration is resulting in many plus benefits for our whole economy; likewise exploration of inner space will bring many plus benefits for the individual.

In this small book some of these benefits have been indicated, but there are others which will be discovered in the "set your feet upon the Moon" segment of your journey.

Reach for the stars in your flight, but enjoy the trip as you go!